D0099778

CALGARY PUBLIC LIBRARY
FISH CREEK AREA LIBRARY

A WEEKEND WITH VAN GOGH

A WEEKEND WITH
VAN GOGH

Text by Rosabianca Skira-Venturi

Translated by Ann Keay Beneduce

RIZZOLI
NEW YORK

*I*t's the
weekend!
Only a week
has passed since I stepped off the
train that brought me from Arles
to Paris, where I hurried to my
brother Theo's apartment. And
there you were, a tiny baby, in your
cradle! I was so happy to see you—
you, the son of my brother whom I
love so much, whose loyalty and belief
in me has made it possible for me to live
and to do my work. During my lifetime I have
written hundreds and hundreds of letters to him,
but now, this weekend, I am writing just to you. I
want to tell you about myself and about my great
work as a painter, so that some day, when you go to
school, you will be proud to say: I am the nephew of

VINCENT VAN GOGH

A halo around the moon in a starry sky.

Right now I am living in Auvers-sur-Oise. It's a village not far from Paris, right in the countryside, with fields of bright yellow wheat and old houses with thatched roofs, as well as some fancier homes, which I also like. I have given your parents a picture, *A Branch of an Almond Tree in Bloom* (page 9), which I painted especially for you; in it I have put all my tenderness and my hope that your life will be beautiful, harmonious, and full of light. My life has not always been like that: I've had some very hard times. But it doesn't matter, for I am convinced that I have done some work that people must respect, whether they like it or not. Today I am tired; I've been ill, but I'll tell you about that later. First, I want you to look carefully at this blossoming almond branch. I know that your parents have hung this canvas above the piano and that it is always near you. That is good, as my style of painting takes a little getting used to. I always use strong colors, so strong they almost scream at each other. In this painting, the vivid blue of the background makes the color of the flowers more brilliant, and the green of the stems and leaves even greener. Sometimes I put a harsh red next to a violent green. These colors are meant to be shocking—I want to make people notice my paintings and look at them with care!

I don't mix colors on my palette; instead, I take a bit of each color separately on my paintbrush and then make dots of it on the canvas, or little swirls or hatch-marks, whatever makes that part of the canvas lively and brings the trees, flowers, stones, and people to life. You have seen the portrait I have done of myself painting,

with my palette held firmly in my hand (*Self-Portrait with Easel,* page 6). Did you notice how I painted my hair? I did it in all colors, even little green dots, and made my beard very red. Looking at this painting, you can tell that I have red hair and a ruddy complexion—and that I am sturdy and broad-shouldered. But you can also see my real nature—which is not always charming—as well as how I go about my profession: passionately, even violently.

10

In Auvers, where I am now living, I have just done a picture showing a corner of the village: a path leads to a staircase which climbs up to some red-roofed houses. As you look at this scene, it seems as if everything in it is on the move. The people's bodies twist as they almost skip along the path, and the rocks and trees take on strange shapes in the strong light. I always paint quickly, for everything can look different a moment later. I feel very strong emotions while I try to capture a living, moving instant—an instant held suspended at the end of my paintbrush. You might say that I paint as if I were fighting a battle against time, which passes all too quickly.

*Theo, my brother,
at about 30 years of age.*

In my letters to your father I often made sketches of what I was working on, with little notes to explain them, sort of like the notations on a piece of music: blue here, green here, and so on. I could picture in my mind the scene I wanted to paint and, as the sketches show, I had already decided on the composition. But painting it was something else entirely. Someday it may amuse you to to compare these sketches with the actual paintings. For instance, what became of the cat in my painting *Springtime* (Page 13)? Let's just say it went back inside that house with the red roof.

Fields of wheat—The Reaper *(this page) and* Wheatfield with Cypress *(page 15).*

My artistic elders, the Impressionists, often painted outdoors, trying to capture and reproduce their immediate sensations or impressions of light and color. So did I. But it is the power of nature that interests me most—I want to paint its vital force. I like to show it close up, almost as if I were painting while lying on the ground. I study the drifting clouds in the sky and gaze at the enormous sun. Look, you can see the twisted trunks of trees amid stalks of wheat bent over by a violent wind, a wind so strong you can almost hear it whistling as you look at my painting. Oh, the wind! The *mistral,* the harsh, strong wind of Provence!

I like to draw with a pen made from a sharpened reed.

But I haven't told you about this yet: I lived for two years in that heat, that brilliant light, and that fierce wind. I lived in Provence, in southern France. If you go to this beautiful area you will certainly recognize the scenes and landscapes that I painted.

Here I am at age 13.

Let's pause for a moment. You must know that I envy your peacefulness as you lie quietly asleep. All that I am saying must mean very little to you right now. But in a few years I'm sure you will understand me. After all, you are named after me. That's not very original, however, as there have been so many Vincents in our family! For example, there was your distinguished great-uncle who made his fortune as a publisher of reproductions of works of art and as an art dealer. As your father will tell you, we come from a hard-working, middle-class Dutch family that had a strong sense of duty to others and felt that human destiny was inevitably tragic. Your grandfather, my father, was a perfect example of this: a deeply religious Protestant, he was appointed pastor, or priest, in a depressed, burned-out region in the north of Holland. I also wanted to become a pastor— can you believe that? For many long months I tried to help the poverty-stricken people in a mining area on the border between France and Belgium, a bleak region, its pale light filled with coal dust from the mines.

The practiced stroke of the reaper.

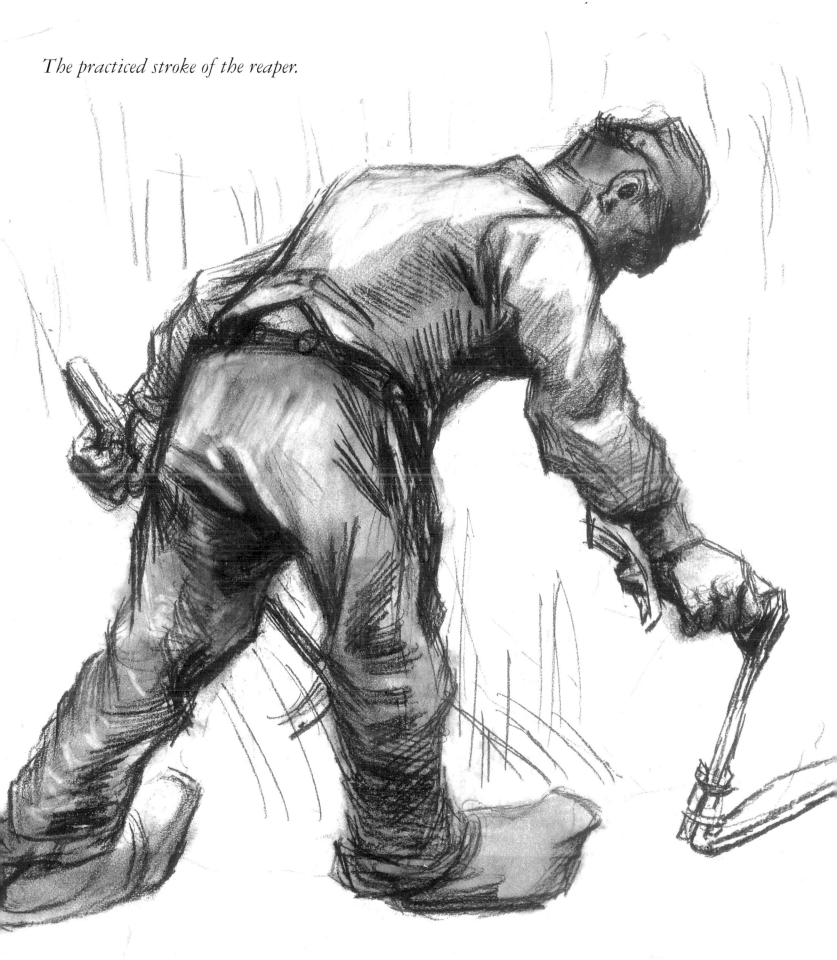

The faces and gestures of these people reminded me of characters described in the Bible. I painted and drew them at their work and at home, using thick, black strokes. "I wanted these pictures to make people think about a way of life very different from that of 'civilized' people like us," I wrote to Theo. "A painting of peasants should smell of lard, of ripened wheat, of apples, even of manure; that's a healthy aroma, especially for city dwellers."

Graphite and black pencil are what I use to draw these workers and their wives at their everyday tasks. This is their country: a land of tall chimneys and mountains of coal.

Living in this region of poor miners and trying as hard as I could to comfort them was so hard for me that finally, exhausted and depressed, I went back to live for a while at my parents' home in Nuenen, Holland. There I did a lot of paintings and drawings of these hard-working people. Using strong black strokes combined with browns and dark tans, I tried to recapture on canvas or paper the heavy atmosphere of their painful existence—no one even spoke at the family dinner table because they were all so worn out from their back-breaking work in the dry earth. Even the sun, when it tried to come out, brought them no pleasure.

There was a garden outside of the rectory where I could dream. I made several drawings of it in pen-and-ink or with a thick black pencil. In one of these you see that I sketched a little black ghost. But don't be afraid, it is really just an accidental inkblot that I turned into something decorative.

But, if one wants to paint, how can one go on living in such a drab light?

Here I am at the age of 18!

A bank of the Seine River, a favorite subject of the Impressionists.

Once more I left home.
And I found myself in Paris.

The interior of a restaurant with flower petals, even on the walls.

Without giving him any advance warning, I rang your father's doorbell. And Theo, though bowled over with surprise, made me welcome there. As he still does today, he worked at an art gallery and also tried to sell my paintings. At that time, Paris seemed a wonderful place. I was filled with inspiration and enthusiasm.

Before long I came to know the whole group of Impressionist painters, some of whom had already become famous and were earning very good livings. Others I knew, from my own generation, had more or less the same difficulties I did: they sold little or nothing and none of them had any money. I had no money either, but I had a marvelous brother.

"Father" Pissarro.

So, Paris for me was full of friends. There was Camille Pissarro, the old patriarch, with his big heart and his flowing beard; he was sympathetic and kind to me. And there was the brilliant Henri de Toulouse-Lautrec, whose growth was stunted as a child—he avenged himself with his cruel paintings and his harsh wit. But Toulouse-Lautrec, though of noble lineage, gave me his friendship even when I was quite a vagabond. And we made very good drinking companions!

The piercing gaze of Cézanne.

Degas, the dandy.

Gauguin, "the king of the Incas."

The elegant, witty Edgar Degas, a wickedly ironic and sensitive genius, gave me some very good advice about painting, and so did the shy, rather grumpy old Paul Cézanne. An innovative younger painter, Georges Seurat, soon had all of us experimenting with his "pointillist" technique, using little dots ("points") of color. But most of all it is Paul Gauguin I should tell you about. A descendant of the Incas—or so he liked to pretend—he was incredibly attractive, with a distinctive profile and a nose bent sharply like the blade of a knife. He charmed and impressed all the young painters, but he was eternally penniless and always complaining!

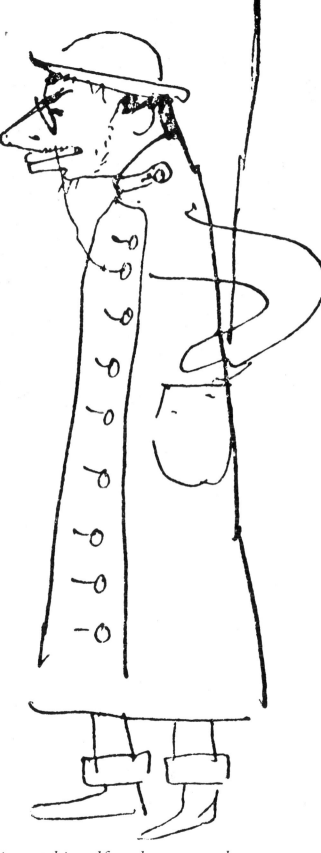

Toulouse-Lautrec played the role of a clown, laughing at himself and everyone else.

View from the window of a café where I often went.

Wouldn't you think I had painted these windmills in Holland? But actually they are in the backyards of Montmartre. Paris still had many charming country corners at that time. I worked hard there, sometimes just painting what I could see from my window. But I also loved painting the wide avenues of Paris leading off into the distance, as well as the banks of the Seine, so dear to the Impressionists. This was a happy period of my life, with lots of visits to the studios of one friend or another, or to a nearby bistro for dinner. For the first time, I began to use bright, strong colors. I combined little dots of color very close together, like Seurat, with wider brushstrokes in such a way that the surface of my canvas almost seemed to be moving. I might paint the interior of a gaslit restaurant, or choose simpler subjects like some books with covers in different shades of yellow, or some apples and oranges placed just so on a flat wicker tray. All of this brought me moments of great joy. From morning to night I painted, quite happy with what I produced and filled with admiration for the work of the other painters.

A friend sketched me painting.

A fashion swept Paris for Japanese woodblock prints at that time; my friends—and I, too—liked them very much. Look at this portrait I made of Père Tanguy. He owned a modest art supply store where many artists went to buy paints and canvases and everything they needed for painting. Although few of us could pay him—myself included—he grumblingly permitted this, whether he liked it or not. The portrait I did of him (in fact, I did two of them) shows him posing as a sailor from Brittany who has just returned from a voyage to the Far East. Behind him, the wall is covered with exotic Japanese prints, setting us to dreaming of faraway places.

Did the poor vagabond I was then become a great painter, well respected in Paris and in his own country? If you said yes, that shows how little you know about me, for I must tell you I eventually ran into a great deal of debt. Theo wasn't able to find buyers for my paintings, so I was totally dependent on him for everything. In fact, I still am to this day! It is a sad and difficult situation for both of us, in spite of the deep affection that binds us and his unwavering belief in me. But let me say this clearly: I am convinced that my painting is good enough to make up for all the hardships Theo and I have had to endure for its sake. I feel this strongly. But what will you think about it, I wonder?

Little by little, I grew tired of Paris. I began to feel rejected by my friends. Always stubborn, I had clung to my ironclad conviction that if we artists, both rich and poor, worked together, we would eventually find public acceptance for our work. But no one really believed this. Everything became more and more difficult. Even the light in Paris began to seem gray to me, always beaded with raindrops!

I dreamed of sun and warmth. And what place could fulfill these dreams as well as Arles, a town in southern France, in the region called Provence?

On Monday, February 20, 1888, I arrived in Arles after more than fifteen hours on the train—only to be met by a snowstorm and freezing temperatures! No one in Provence could remember such bad weather! And it lasted more than two weeks. And then, when the snow stopped falling and the ice began to melt a little, the *mistral,* the region's famous harsh wind, began to blow. But it didn't matter! I had made up my mind to stay there and settle down. I worked in Provence for more than two years. I did many, many paintings and drawings there. Sometimes my life there was very happy—but I also had some terrible experiences.

Arles, in sunlight.

In spite of everything, I love this part of the country. The fields lie open to the eye for great distances; huge haystacks gleam like gold in the sunlight; the sky, swept by the *mistral,* is by turns tormented and clear; the air is so transparent that each blade of grass looks crisp and bright; and the water looks sometimes like a diamond, sometimes like an emerald.

The people here are also stunning— strong characters, with unexpected attitudes and original ideas, and a high-spiritedness that made me feel happy, too.

Naturally everyone used to gather in the courtyard of the inn where the stagecoaches stopped. All kinds of people would cram themselves together in these vehicles for the trip to the little town of Tarascon, about thirty-five miles away. These coaches were painted in bright colors—red, blue, and yellow—that sparkled against a patch of blue sky. This is how I showed them in a picture I painted very quickly. They reminded me of an amusing book I had just read, *Tartarin de Tarascon,* by Alphonse Daudet, the famous writer of Provence. The story includes a talking stagecoach: "It was an old-fashioned stagecoach, upholstered in the traditional manner with

Riding on a donkey up to Alphonse Daudet's windmill in Fontvielle.

bright blue cloth, now rather faded, and trimmed with enormous rough wool pompoms," wrote Daudet. I can't tell you the whole story here, but do read it when you are older, you will enjoy it. The lament of this rickety old coach, deported to Africa because it was better than nothing, will surely make you smile as you look at my picture. On my canvas, too, it has a plaintive, winded look. Yet here it goes to only a few places, peacefully crossing the level plain alongside the foothills of the Alps—nothing like torrid Africa!

After several days of living in café-hotels where the bad cooking upset my stomach, I rented a little house (*The Yellow House, right*). I wanted to paint my room, get some furniture, install gas heating—in short, to make it a welcoming place for friends to come and visit. It would also be a studio for me to paint in and a place to exhibit my work.

Since I was painting everything around me, I made these paintings of the corner of the street with the yellow house and also my room (*The Bedroom, right*).

I have painted myself once again. "I have tried to keep it simple," I wrote to Theo, "but the colors… are very acid."

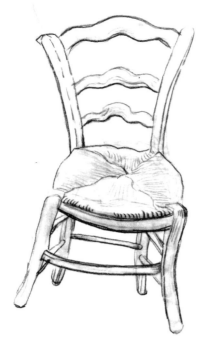

As I see it, I feel that in this painting I have succeeded in conveying a feeling of peace and restfulness with the fresh, bright colors of the walls, the furniture and all the objects in the room. The blinds are closed against the hot sunlight, everything is in order. I only have to slip into my nice bed to get the rest I need so much.

Everyone is enchanted by the beauty of Arles and the surrounding countryside. The fields, carefully plowed and neatly fenced, the trees, the flowers—blue irises, yellow sunflowers—their impact sent me flying to my canvas or drawing paper, or set me to writing endless letters to your father.

On the plain of Crau, near Arles, the market-gardeners tend their small gardens.

The ruins of the abbey at Montmajour.

I loved to take long hikes and little trips to the surrounding areas. After a trip to the ancient abbey of Montmajour, I wrote to Theo, "I've just come back from a trip to Montmajour. I explored the old garden and stole some excellent figs. The big rosebushes; the pomegranate trees with their fat, bright orange fruits; the hundred-year-old cypresses; willows, ash, and oaks; half-demolished stairways; arched windows in ruins; lichen-covered blocks of white stone; sections of crumbling walls here and there among the greenery." You can see the abbey in the distance at the upper-left of my painting, *Le Crau* (page 36).

To me, in June, everything looks golden—the haystacks, of course, but also the houses.

There are plenty of places in Arles where you would want to take a leisurely walk, or perhaps sit and read the newspaper. The famous Alyscamps promenade is one of these, with its series of old Roman and Christian tombs in what is now a public park. I have painted this scene several times in warm, autumn tones (*Alyscamps*, page 39).

I have mentioned to you how amazing the people are here: the women are remarkably beautiful in their characteristic costumes; wearing white scarves and crowned with traditional headdresses they look like queens. I had Madame Ginoux, who owns the Café de la Gare, pose for me. "It is a portrait I painted in three-quarters of an hour—background pale yellow, skin grayish, dress black, black, black with some raw Prussian blue. She leans upon a green table and is sitting in an orange wooden chair." That is how I described it in a letter to your father. These words show you how eager I was to make a powerful painting: I put the colors directly onto the canvas, just as they came out of the tubes, without mixing, almost as if I were cutting them out of colored paper.

41

However, despite these successes, I still felt nervous and anxious—even my Sunflowers and the Irises that I loved to paint seemed to have tormented souls under my paintbrush. But then, after lots of coaxing and persuasion on my part, Paul Gauguin finally decided to join me in Arles, although he had all sorts of misgivings, not only about finances. He arrived on October 23, 1888, and we spent two months together.

Gauguin set to work at once. Like me, he painted the Alyscamps, Madame Ginoux, and the interior of a café. We also spent lots of time strolling around, talking about painting, of the best way—the only way, according to us—of making the public understand and appreciate the strong and unconventional sensations that we wanted to express in our art. These discussions were pleasant and I found them very comforting at first. But after a while I realized that something was beginning to go wrong. I could no longer feel the warmth of real friendship within Gauguin's attitude; always haughty, he now seemed withdrawn and tense. And it seemed to me that he wanted me to submit completely to his theories, his tastes, his choices—even culinary ones! I felt my spirit being crushed. One evening, after a violent argument between us, in a fit of rage I cut off one of my earlobes. Bleeding, I rushed out, but then had to come back to my room and lie down. I don't remember anything more. Theo, told of this catastrophe by Gauguin, came as quickly as he could—it was Christmas Eve—and I awoke to find myself in the hospital in Arles.

I painted this portrait of myself, with my bandaged head, six days after leaving the hospital (*Self-Portrait, Man with a Pipe*). It can tell you more than many big words about what had happened to me. My eyes say that, although sad, I was still confident in myself. Sad, I might well be! My beautiful dream of a life shared with my friend and fellow artist, in both work and hardship, had vanished into thin air. Some of my own behavior had sown the seeds of panic in the arrogant Gauguin and he had taken cowardly flight.

But I stood firm, still believing in myself. My ability to paint was not damaged; perhaps it was even stronger than ever, and that is why—look at me carefully—I could sit there calmly smoking my pipe. My mind was made up! I would stay on in the south of France and keep on working as hard as ever.

Well, here we are at the end of the weekend. Surely you must be asleep in your cradle by now, and I am tired, too. Night is falling and I still want to write to your father, wonderful Theo who, in all the storms and squalls of life, has never let me down. He has always understood me and I know he always will. Now it is nearly dark. Before coming to see you, while I was still in Arles, I painted a picture that I like very much, and I'd like you to look at it. It is called *The Starry Night.* In the picture it is dark, but the lights of the village are reflected in the water. Overhead, brilliant stars seem to sweep across the sky in a great, dazzling movement. These same stars will help me find my own peace. I know, too, that they will pass on to you my absolute confidence in my painting, my art. For, believe me, art is magic.

The baby who was sleeping so peacefully in his cradle became an engineer and a great man when he grew up. Little by little, he came to look surprisingly like his uncle—an uncle who, nervously exhausted and at the end of his strength, fled into a wheatfield one morning to end his own life. Vincent, the nephew, knew very well that "art is magic." He passionately loved his uncle's paintings. Better still, he knew how to share this love. He created a splendid museum where everyone can see a great collection of the masterpieces painted by his uncle, who, in turn, would have said, "I am proud of you." He wrote:

The work of Vincent van Gogh reflects human dignity. It is as if he wanted to say through his painting that, if we work at it with enough good will, we will someday be able to appreciate how beautiful the world is and what a good place it can be in which to live.

WHERE TO SEE VAN GOGH

Although van Gogh was almost totally unknown and unappreciated during his lifetime, his works are now among the most visited and admired of any artist. His paintings and drawings are distributed throughout the world, with some of his greatest works here in the United States. You can see his works in the following places:

UNITED STATES
New York

Next to the Van Gogh Museum in Amsterdam, New York City is home to more of van Gogh's great works than any other city.

On Fifth Avenue, at the edge of Central Park, stands the huge Metropolitan Museum of Art. Their wonderful collection of European paintings includes a whole roomful of van Gogh paintings! Here you'll see *Cypresses, Still Life with Irises,* one of his *Sunflowers,* his *Self-Portrait with Straw Hat, Irises* (page 43), and *The Arlesian, Portrait of Madame Ginoux* (page 41). The Met also owns several of his drawings and watercolors, including a marvelous version of *The Zouave.*

A few blocks north of the Met is the distinctive building designed by Frank Lloyd Wright housing the Guggenheim Museum. The Guggenheim has a few choice paintings by van Gogh, including *Mountains at Saint-Rémy* and *The Viaduct,* as well as some drawings.

At The Museum of Modern Art, in midtown Manhattan, you can see one of the artist's masterpieces—*The Starry Night* (a detail is on page 8; another version is on page 47). The museum also owns a few works on paper, including *Corridor in the Asylum* and *Street in Saintes-Maries-de-la-Mer.*

You'll also want to go to the Brooklyn Museum. There you can see a *Self-Portrait* and several of his drawings, including a wonderful pen-and-ink version of the Met's *Cypresses.*

Washington, D.C.

On the mall near the U.S. Capitol in Washington is the National Gallery of Art. Here you will find *Farmhouse in Provence* and *La Mousmé*, a Japanese-style portrait of a girl from Provence. Not far away, in the Phillips Collection, there are several important van Gogh paintings, including *Entrance to the Park* and *The Road Menders*. You can also see van Gogh's drawing of *The Moulin de la Galette* ("The windmill of the Galette," a popular dance hall in Paris).

Connecticut

The Yale University Art Gallery in New Haven has *The Night Café*.

Massachusetts

The collection of the Museum of Fine Arts, Boston, has a great number of Impressionist works, with several works by van Gogh. Among them are *Portrait of Joseph Roulin* and *La Berceuse,* and some of his early paintings, like *Weaver with Bobbin Winder,* which he painted in 1884.

The Fogg Art Museum at Harvard University owns the spectacular *Self-Portrait* on page 34, *Three Pairs of Shoes,* and several of his drawings.

Pennsylvania

At the Philadelphia Museum of Art you can see one of van Gogh's famous paintings of *Sunflowers*. The museum also has several of his drawings; be sure to see the marvelous *Haystacks*.

Illinois

Near the lakefront of Chicago, on Michigan Avenue, you'll find the Art Institute of Chicago. One of the first collections of modern art in America, the museum owns a version of *The Bedroom* (page 35) as well as the painting *Public Garden with Weeping Tree*. The Institute also has some important drawings, such as a pencil-and-pen *Cypresses* and a *Self-Portrait*.

Maryland

When you're in Baltimore, be sure to go to the Baltimore Museum of Art, where you'll find the painting *A Pair of Shoes,* as well as several drawings.

Texas

The Museum of Fine Arts in Houston owns *Rocks with Oak Tree.*

California

In Southern California, head to the Los Angeles County Museum of Art, which stands next to the La Brea Tar Pits. Inside you'll find several van Gogh drawings, including *Portrait of Joseph Roulin* and *The Langlois Bridge.*

A little east of Los Angeles is the Norton Simon Museum of Art in Pasadena, whose marvelous collection includes van Gogh's *Portrait of Patience Escalier.*

Missouri

At the Nelson-Atkins Museum of Art in Kansas City you can see two van Gogh paintings, *Olive Grove* and *Head of a Peasant.*

THE NETHERLANDS
Amsterdam

To really get to know van Gogh, you should visit the Van Gogh Museum in Amsterdam. Housed in a very modern building, open to the outdoors, it has vast interior spaces on several levels. Here, in a warm and welcoming light, the pictures almost seem to talk to one another. Situated a little outside of the city, it contains the prestigious collection that the engineer Vincent van Gogh, the painter's beloved nephew, put together so that they could be seen and studied together: two hundred paintings, 550 drawings, and seven hundred letters! The collection is comprehensive, ranging from his earliest drawings to his last paintings. There are too many great works here to list—highlights include *Self-Portrait with Easel* (page 6), *Branch of an Almond Tree in Bloom* (page 9), *The Bedroom* (page 35), and *Sunflowers* (page 42).

The Stedelijk Museum in Amsterdam has several van Goghs—a trip here will let you see *Allotments on Montmartre* and a version of *La Berceuse.*

Otterlo

The State Museum Kröller-Müller in Otterlo also has many great works by van Gogh, from his earliest paintings to those he made at the end of his life. Here you can find *Interior of a Restaurant* (page 23), *Peach Trees in Blossom,* and *The Sower* (cover), to name just a few.

FRANCE
Paris

Paris is the third city—after Amsterdam and New York—where you can see a great number of van Gogh's masterpieces. The Musée d'Orsay, housed in a magnificent old train station along the Seine River, contains a vast collection of art from the 19th and early 20th centuries. The museum has nineteen paintings by van Gogh; among them are *Starry Night* (page 47), a *Self-Portrait* full of swirls, *Portrait of Doctor Gachet,* a third version of *The Bedroom,* and a version of *The Arlesian, Portrait of Madame Ginoux.*

In Paris you'll also want to go to the Musée Rodin, devoted to the sculpture of Auguste Rodin. The museum houses much of Rodin's art collection and includes van Gogh's *Portrait of Père Tanguy* (page 28).

IMPORTANT DATES IN THE LIFE OF VAN GOGH

1853   Vincent van Gogh was born on March 30 in Zundert, in the south of Holland, near the Belgian frontier. It was a depressed area where the peasants and other workers barely eked out a painful existence. Vincent's father was a pastor in this predominantly Protestant region. The van Gogh family was an old, well-established one. Middle-class, pious, and strict, but also entrepreneurial, the family included priests, sailors, businessmen, and art lovers. Three of Vincent's uncles were art dealers.

1857   Birth of Theo, the brother with whom Vincent exchanged a great number of letters throughout his life. It was Theo who, generous and patient and a constant believer in Vincent's talent, sent him the money he needed in order to live and paint. Vincent had another brother and three sisters, but he did not relate well to the rest of his family. He was a solitary, dreamy child with short-cropped red hair and a bony, serious face. He loved to wander alone in the moors and heaths of his low-lying country, Holland.

1865–1869   Vincent lived in boarding schools, where he was very unhappy. In 1869 his parents sent him to the Hague to be a salesman at the Goupil art gallery, a branch of a gallery in Paris. A model employee, young Vincent was sent to work in the London office, with occasional stays in Paris.

1875   In May, Vincent was transferred to the gallery's main office in Paris, but he felt lonely and distraught there. He read the Bible constantly and little else seemed to have any meaning for him. Finally, he quit his job at Goupil and left Paris.

1876–1880   He returned to England. After a period as a master in a dreary school, he became assistant preacher in a Protestant Methodist parish in one of the most miserable suburbs of London. Hoping to become a pastor, he went back to the University of Amsterdam, and later to Brussels, but he failed and gave up his studies. He took a voluntary position in an evangelist mission to help the miners in Borinage, a sad, poverty-stricken area of Belgium, with gray light and huge black mountains of coal. Drawn to them by pity, he cared for, comforted, and encouraged these workers with a devotion that overtaxed his own strength. But, though dedicated, he was not a gifted speaker and the Church did not renew his contract. So he was once again without work, a homeless wanderer.

In 1880, after a long silence between the two brothers, Vincent sent a long letter to Theo begging him to "see in him something other than the worst sort of idler." Theo assured him of his belief in him. Soon afterwards, Vincent wrote him anew: "And yet in this terrible misery I feel my energy reviving…I will pick up my pencil, which I had put down in discouragement, and will begin to draw again." And from that time on, this was the road he would follow.

1881–
1885
Vincent was already deeply committed to painting and had visited the great museums in Paris, London, and Amsterdam. To learn perspective and anatomy, he apprenticed himself to a master painter in Brussels; then he went to the Hague to study with Anton Mauve, a well-known painter at that time. In 1883 he went back to live with his parents in Nuenen, constantly drawing and planning great paintings. In dark lines and somber colors he did a series of paintings of the local peasants and workers at their daily tasks, capturing their natural expressions and gestures. In 1885, his father died suddenly. Not long after this, Vincent enrolled at the Academy of Fine Arts in Anvers, where his work was not appreciated.

1886–
1887
Abruptly, in the beginning of 1886, Vincent decided to leave for Paris. Theo, though a bit disconcerted, made him welcome at his apartment in Montmartre, a section of Paris where many artists lived. Theo was the director of an art gallery where, in the basement,

he occasionally exhibited the work of the Impressionist painters, whom the public still did not appreciate very much. He was eventually very successful in selling these works, but never the work of his brother.

Vincent now found himself in Paris among all the young and not-so-young artists who would become very well known a few decades later. They worked, they met, they fraternized, and they gave each other helpful criticism. Vincent made many drawings and over two hundred paintings: landscapes, portraits, flowers and still lifes. His colors were bright, sometimes violent. He always wanted to help his companions, so he tried (without much success) to arrange exhibitions of their work in cafés. And everywhere he proclaimed his idea for an artists' union, which no one really wanted. Finally, Paris became too difficult for him—the light too gray and the weather too rainy—so he decided to leave. He chose the south of France, where he was sure the sun would do him good and he would be able to have a studio, perhaps together with other artists.

1888   He settled down in Arles, first in a room above a restaurant, later in a little white studio in a yellow house. From spring to winter, day and night, Vincent drew and painted: the countryside, the planted fields, the plain that extended to the foothills of the Alps, the glorious sunflowers, the irises, the fields of wheat—a world wide open to the burning sun and the region's intense winds. In spite of a certain reserve on the part of the people there, he formed friendships, especially with the family of the postman, who helped him through some difficult moments.

Always he wrote to Theo, sometimes twice a day. Theo sent him money to live on and paints and canvas, and Vincent told him in minute detail about his work, and also about his ever-present idea for an artists' colony. His friend from Paris, Paul Gauguin, seemed restless—he should come to Arles, wrote Vincent. At the end of October, Gauguin arrived. The artists shared two months of communal life, which began with rambles in the countryside and ended in tragedy. One day, driven to distraction by Gauguin's arrogance, Vincent tried to hit him. Then, running outside, he cut off one of his own earlobes. Unconscious, he was taken to the hospital. Gauguin left. Theo came to help Vincent.

1889   After two months in the hospital, Vincent came home. He began to work again, making a lot of drawings and many paintings. But he was exhausted, and his increasingly strange behavior eventually disturbed his neighbors in Arles, who called the police. After a short stay in the hospital in Arles, he asked to be admitted to the asylum in Saint-Rémy, a small town nearby. There he had two rooms and, as much as possible, he continued to paint.

1890   In January the first enthusiastic and appreciative article about his painting was published, and several months later one of his paintings—probably the only one during his lifetime—was sold.

But the big event for Vincent was the birth of a son to Theo and his wife Jo, whom Vincent described as "charming, simple and affectionate." So in May Vincent came to Paris and "silently, with tears in his eyes, kissed the baby who bore his own name as the infant lay in his cradle." Vincent also saw some of his old friends. However, he still preferred to live in the country. He found a place in Auvers, near Paris, where he could be under the care of Dr. Gachet, who was not only a doctor but also an amateur painter, an art collector, and a friend of artists. Vincent continued to paint with passion and fervor; he especially loved the "fields of wheat spread out beneath the troubled skies." It was in the middle of one of these fields that, on July 27, he took his own life.

He was only thirty-seven years old, and yet he had left the world an enormous legacy—a body of uniquely beautiful creations. Six months later his favorite brother Theo also died. The two brothers now lie side-by-side in the small cemetery in Auvers-sur-Oise.

LIST OF ILLUSTRATIONS

The following is a list of the titles and locations for works of art reproduced in this book. A work's dimensions are given in both inches and centimeters, first by height, then by width.

Pages 4–5
View of Arles (detail), May 1888. Reed pen and sepia ink. Rhode Island School of Design Museum of Art, Providence, Rhode Island.

Page 6
Self-Portrait with Easel, 1888. Oil on canvas, 25¾ × 19⅞" (65.5 cm × 50.5 cm). Van Gogh Museum, Amsterdam.

Page 7
Flowering tendril, 1890. Pen and ink wash, 18¾ × 15¾" (47.5 × 40 cm). Van Gogh Museum, Amsterdam (Museum photo).

Page 8
The Starry Night (detail), June 1889. Oil on canvas, 29 × 36¼" (73.7 × 92.1 cm). The Museum of Modern Art, New York.

Page 9
Branch of an Almond Tree in Bloom, February 1890. Oil on canvas, 28¾ × 36¼" (73 × 92 cm). Van Gogh Museum, Amsterdam.

Pages 10–11
The Staircase at Auvers, June 1890. Oil on canvas, 20 × 28" (50.8 × 71.1 cm). City Art Museum, St. Louis, Missouri.

Page 12
Sketch of *Springtime* on letter to Theo, April 20, 1888. Pen. Van Gogh Museum, Amsterdam.

Photograph of Theo, around the age of 30.

Flowering Border of a Garden, 1888. Reed pen, 24 × 19¼" (61 × 49 cm). Van Gogh Museum, Amsterdam (Museum photo).

Page 13
Springtime (Fruit Trees in Bloom, House), 1888. Oil on canvas, 24 × 22⅞" (72 × 58 cm). Private collection, Switzerland.

Page 14
The Reaper, June 1889. Oil on canvas, 28¾ × 36¼" (73 × 92 cm). Van Gogh Museum, Amsterdam.

Page 15
A Farm in Provence (detail), n.d. Graphite, sharpened-reed pen, and sepia ink on vellum. Van Gogh Museum, Amsterdam (Museum photo).

Wheatfield and Cypress, June 1889. Oil on canvas, 28½ × 36" (72.5 × 91.5 cm). National Gallery, London.

Page 16
Photograph of Vincent in 1866.

Page 17
Farmer Reaping, Back View, 1885. Black pencil, 16½ × 20¼" (42 × 52 cm). Van Gogh Muscum, Amsterdam (Muscum photo).

Page 18
Head of a Peasant, 1885. Graphite, 13¾ × 8½" (35 × 21.5 cm). Van Gogh Museum, Amsterdam (Museum photo).

Postcard of the colliery at Cuesmes.

Page 20
Woman Shelling Peas, 1885. Black pencil, 16½ × 10¼" (42 × 26 cm). Van Gogh Museum, Amsterdam (Museum photo).

Page 21
Rectory Garden in Winter, 1884. Pen and graphite, 15⅜ × 20⅞" (39 × 53 cm). Van Gogh Museum, Amsterdam (Museum photo).

Page 23
Interior of a Restaurant, 1887. Oil on canvas, 17¾ × 22¼" (45 × 56.5 cm). Kröller-Müller Museum, Otterlo, The Netherlands.

Page 24
Camille Pissarro (1830–1903) in his studio at Eragny, c. 1884.

Paul Cézanne (1839–1906), *Self-Portrait,* 1880–82. Pencil. Private collection.

Marcellin Desboutin (1823–1902), *Portrait of Degas,* c. 1876. Etching. Bibliothèque Nationale, Paris.

Page 25
Paul Gauguin (1848–1903), *Self-Portrait* (detail). Charcoal and colored pencils. Drawing Collection, Louvre, Paris, France.

Henri de Toulouse-Lautrec (1864–1901), *Caricatured Self-Portrait,* 1885. Pencil, $6^{7}/_{8} \times 4^{1}/_{2}$" (17.5 × 11.5 cm). Musée Toulouse-Lautrec, Albi, France.

Page 26
The Window of the Restaurant Bataille, 1887. Pen and colored pencils, $21 \times 15^{1}/_{2}$" (53.5 × 39.5 cm). Van Gogh Museum, Amsterdam (Museum photo).

Pages 26–27
Kitchen Gardens at Montmartre: La Butte Montmartre, c. 1887. Oil on canvas, $37^{3}/_{4} \times 47^{1}/_{4}$" (96 × 120 cm). Stedelijk Museum, Amsterdam.

Page 28
Le Père Tanguy, 1887–88. Oil on canvas, $36^{1}/_{4} \times 28^{3}/_{4}$" (92 × 73 cm). Musée Rodin, Paris.

Page 29
Emile Bernard (1868-1941), *Van Gogh Painting,* 1887. Pencil, $5^{3}/_{4} \times 5^{1}/_{2}$" (14.5 × 14 cm). Private collection.

Pages 30–31
Roger Viollet, *Arles, general view of the arenas.*

Page 32
Roger Viollet, *Arles, the plaza of the Forum.*

Page 33
Landscape With the Windmill of Alphonse Daudet at Fontvielle, 1888. Graphite and reed pen with brown ink, $10 \times 13^{1}/_{2}$" (25.5 × 34.5 cm). Van Gogh Museum, Amsterdam (Museum photo).

Page 33
The Stagecoaches of Tarascon, 1888. Oil on canvas, 28¾ × 36¼" (72 × 92 cm). The Henry and Rose Pearlman Foundation, Inc.

Page 34
Self-Portrait, 1888. Oil on canvas, 23⅝ × 19⅝" (60 × 49.9 cm). Fogg Art Museum, Harvard University, Cambridge, Massachusetts.

Page 34
The Yellow House, 1888. Watercolor, 10⅛ × 12½" (25.7 × 31.7 cm). Van Gogh Museum, Amsterdam.

Page 35
The Chair, 1888. Oil on canvas, 13 × 9⅞" (33 × 25 cm). Van Gogh Museum, Amsterdam.

The Bedroom, 1888. Oil on canvas, 28⅜ × 35½" (72 × 90 cm). Van Gogh Museum, Amsterdam.

Page 36
La Crau, the Gardens of the Market-farmers, June 1888. Oil on canvas, 28⅜ × 36¼" (72 × 92 cm). Van Gogh Museum, Amsterdam.

Page 37
Roger Viollet, *Montmajour, ruins of the Benedictine abbey of Saint-Pierre de Montmajour.*

Page 38
Haystacks in Provence, June 1888. Oil on canvas, 28¾ × 36¼" (73 × 92.5 cm). Kröller-Müller Museum, Otterlo, The Netherlands.

Page 39
The Alyscamps, October 1888. Oil on canvas, 36⅝ × 28⅜" (93 × 72 cm). Private collection, Lausanne, Switzerland.

Page 40
Roger Viollet, *Arlesian women in traditional costume, early 20th century.*

Page 41
The Arlesian, Portrait of Madame Ginoux, November 1888. Oil on canvas, 36 × 29" (91.4 × 73.7 cm). Metropolitan Museum of Art, New York.

Page 42

Sunflowers, August 1888. Oil on canvas, 27¾ × 29⅛" (96 × 74 cm). Van Gogh Museum, Amsterdam.

Page 43

Irises, 1890. Oil on canvas, 28¾ × 36⅝" (73 × 93 cm). Metropolitan Museum of Art, New York.

Page 45

Self-Portrait, Man With a Pipe, January–February 1889. Oil on canvas, 20 × 17¾" (51 × 45 cm). Private collection.

Page 47

Starry Night, September 1888. Oil on canvas, 28½ × 36¼" (72.5 × 92 cm). Musée d'Orsay, Paris, France (on loan).

First published in the United States of America in 1994 by
Rizzoli International Publications, Inc.
300 Park Avenue South
New York, New York 10010

Copyright © 1993 Editions d'Art Albert Skira, S.A.
English translation copyright © 1994 Rizzoli International Publications, Inc.

All rights reserved. No part of this publication may be reproduced in any form
whatsoever without written permission from the publisher.

Library of Congress Cataloging-in-Publication Data

Skira-Venturi, Rosabianca.
    [Dimanche avec Van Gogh. English]
    A Weekend with Van Gogh / by Rosabianca Skira-Venturi; translated by Ann
Keay Beneduce.
        p. cm.
    ISBN 0-8478-1836-5
    1. Gogh, Vincent van, 1853–1890—Juvenile literature. 2. Painters—Netherlands—
Biography—Juvenile literature. [1. Gogh, Vincent van, 1853–1890. 2. Artists.]
    I. Title.
    ND653.G7S44813 1994
    759.9492—dc20   94-16262
                                                             CIP
                                                             AC

Design by Mary McBride
Printed in Singapore